# *fearLESS*

## A 21 Day Devotional to Feed Your Faith

*Shauna F. King*

*In memory of*

*my best friend, DeAnna*

*who, through all of life's challenges, lived a fearless life.*

# Contents

# Foreword

For the past 7 years, I have had the privilege of serving as Shauna F. King's pastor. Because we serve a God of "connections," I met Shauna's husband, Mark (prior to their marriage), 22 years ago. Little did I know what the Lord was setting in motion. When the King family first visited our church in 2013 through the evangelistic efforts of one of our youth, not only was I excited to see Mark, but I discerned very quickly upon meeting his wife, Shauna, that she was a uniquely gifted and talented woman of God. After becoming members of our church family, Shauna began serving in several capacities. She showed herself to be an extraordinary leader, a wonderful teacher, and an excellent director/producer for our Drama Ministry. The Lord continued to use Shauna mightily in the ensuing years as she was called and commissioned into the preaching ministry in 2018.

Perhaps the greatest Spirit-Inspired Gift I have noticed in Minister Shauna over the years that augment all her giftedness, however, is her ability to encourage. My sentiments will become more apparent as you read her Devotional Book that you now hold, "fearLESS: A 21 Day Devotional." Simply put, if you are dealing with any type of fear, anxiety, worry, or concerns (and we all do from time to time), this Devotional Guide is for you. In this 21 Day Journey, Min. Shauna, in an unbelievably transparent fashion, reveals the power, presence, and promises of God in a refreshing way that is sure to connect with you. As a former schoolteacher and principal who now has an international and national educational training and consulting business, Min. Shauna makes each daily devotion interesting, inspiring, and informative.

If you are like me, you will sometimes start a book but not finish it. I want to encourage you not only to begin "fearLESS: A 21 Day Devotional," but, as the Apostle Paul says, "finish the course." It will change your life!

**Rev. Howard K. Hammond**
Senior Pastor
Springdale Community Church
Springdale, Maryland
November 2020

# Introduction

"The first step in becoming FEARLESS is learning how to fear less." - Shauna King

I feel I need to start this book with a disclaimer. I am not an expert on fear; unless you consider that I have experienced plenty of it as a qualifier. There have been times when my level of fear has paralyzed me or left me with lasting regrets. The truth is, while writing this book, fear often crept in my mind and whispered and even yelled at me, saying, "Who are you to write a book on fear? I started and stopped writing the manuscript too many times to mention.

**"For God has not given us the spirit of fear, but of power, and of love, and of a sound mind."**
**(2 Timothy 1:7 NKJV)**

I have been immensely helped by Scripture, God's very breathed-out Word reveals who He is and provides inspiration and direction. When it comes to fear, I had an interesting relationship with the scripture that tell us that God did not give us the spirit of fear. When I read 2 Timothy 1:7, I felt more challenged than strengthened. It did not provide me with assurance because I felt it questioned my faith. I have dealt with fear for much of my life. As a child, I was afraid of the dark, large dogs, roller coasters, and every horror movie ever shown. I wondered, if God did not give me the spirit of fear, where did my fears come from? Do I lack faith because I struggle with fear? As I have grown in my faith, I have seen how many of my fears have faded, yet others have surfaced. The power that fear had over my life frustrated me so that I knew that I had to make a change. I declared that I was tired of being a "*scare-d-cat*" and that I would learn to let 2 Timothy 1:7 strengthen me. I started with a commitment to daily devotional time to discover the source of my fears and how to trust God through them. Today, I cannot say that all my fears are gone, yet I can confidently say that I no longer let fear dictate my every move.

Devotion, which is an intentional time in meditation and prayer, is a powerful and effective way to connect with God. I began my devotional journey in the book of Psalms and discovered that true freedom from fear comes as we trust in the God who shields us (3:3), protects us (23:4), covers us (91:4), and delivers us from our fears (34:4). Faith and fear have something in common. They both require us to believe something that we cannot see. Although I still have plenty of fear to overcome, I believe that the presence of fear does not equate to a lack of faith. Fear is not good or bad; it just is, and how we respond to it determines its impact.

Twenty-one days is the number of days many believe it takes to form a new habit. The goal with each daily devotion is for fear to begin to lose its power in your life. My commitment to daily devotion helped me to discover the source of my fears. They often stemmed from my environment, my experiences, or even my ego. I am excited to have you to join me for the next 21 days as we feed our faith and starve our fears. I pray God will bless you as you honor Him with your time each day.

**Let's Do This!**


*Shauna*

# Day 1

## TOPIC: THE FIRST STEP

**Key Verse**: Psalm 139:23 "Search me, God, and know my heart; test me and know my anxious thoughts."

At several points in my life, I have been a member of various weight loss programs. While they may have been different in their approach to losing weight, all programs started with the question: What is your current weight? "That dreaded moment when I had to step on the scale. It was a painful yet necessary step. Why was this so important? Because if we do not know our starting point, we cannot identify growth or improvement. The scale put me in a place of honesty and acceptance of what I was carrying.

In Psalm 139:23, I envision David stepping on another type of scale. He is asking God to evaluate his heart. He was crying out to God to search him and to examine his thoughts. He opened himself up to God, who he knew was aware of his "anxious thoughts." David does not pretend to have it all together, but he bows before God and asks the Lord to "examine him and look at his heart." What are your anxious thoughts?

In Spring of 2020, when the COVID-19 pandemic became the #1 news story on every channel, my fears were fueled. Would I contract the virus? Would my loved ones be able to survive if they contracted the virus? With schools and businesses closed indefinitely, would my business fail? Headline after headline predicted: **This will be bad.** I cannot find any other way to describe it other than...I WAS AFRAID. My anxious thoughts were keeping me up at night, and I was not alone. Anxiety about the disease and the short and long-term implications of this pandemic was overwhelming for many people. For most people, fear slowly began to decrease, but for others, a level of fear continued or even consumed their daily lives.

How is fear impacting your life? It may or may not be connected to a pandemic, but you may have other types of fear. Does anxiety and worry impact your daily activities? How has fear affected you in the past month, week, or 24 hours? Webster's dictionary defines the word fearless as *lacking all fear,* but I look at the word in a different way. I see the word as a directive. Fear **Less**. Instead of an unrealistic goal of lacking **all** fear, my goal was to lessen the amount of fear and to minimize its impact on my life. The first step to becoming fearless was learning to fear less.

**Prayer**: *Lord, show me how fear causes me to be less than my best for You. Guide me as I commit to eliminating its negative impact on my life.*

## *fearLESS Thoughts*

*Does the presence of fear mean that you lack faith? How do you respond when you are afraid?*

_____

_____

_____

_____

_____

_____

_____

_____

_____

# Day 2

# TOPIC: AN HONEST HEART

**Key Verse:** Psalm 139:1-2 *"You have searched me; Lord and You know me. You know when I sit and when I rise; You perceive my thoughts from afar."*

Occasionally, I hear one of our children call out for my husband or me in the middle of the night. I can tell by the sound of their voice that something has frightened or scared them. As loving parents, we run to their room and ask them, "What's wrong?" We want to know the source of their fear to understand how we can help. Even though we have said to them, there is no need to be afraid of the dark, we know that sometimes their room may create scary images at night. We do not expect them to tell us what they think we want to hear or that they are not *really* afraid. We know that fear has entered their minds, and honesty is what we expect from them.

Everyone experiences fear. No matter how level-headed or super-spiritual some say they are, we all encounter some level of fear at various points in our lives. The question is not do we experience fear, but how do we respond to fear? Do we operate in fear, hide our fears, or honestly reveal our fears to God? Nothing is hidden from God. He is omniscient or all-knowing. I wonder how often God watches His children as we struggle with our fears, wanting nothing more than to comfort us. But we think, "no, I can do it myself," or "I shouldn't be fearful, so I'm going to act like I am not?" God does not call us to be pretenders. He perceives our thoughts from afar. Therefore, we should remember that the Lord knows everything about us, even when we are afraid.

Dishonesty is born out of fear. Think about it. Whenever you have thought about being dishonest with someone, it was because you *were* afraid *to* be honest with them. One of the first steps on this journey to living a fearless life is to be honest with yourself and with God. God is looking for an honest, intimate relationship with us. Honestly, sharing our fears in prayer instead of pretending they do not exist is a humble act of submission. Allow the Lord to access your inner thoughts. He can handle our doubts and fears better than anyone can, including ourselves. Be honest with Him about how you are feeling. Talk to Him! *"Lord, I am afraid of losing my job," "Lord, I am afraid of what the doctor will say," "Lord, I'm afraid of the path my child is on."* Today, open your heart to God and commit to stop hiding your fears from Him. It is a futile task anyway.

**Prayer**: *Lord, you know me better than I know myself. There is no need to attempt to hide anything from You. I surrender my thoughts to You.*

## *fearLESS Thoughts*

Are you afraid of being honest with God? Tell God the "whole story" about something that has you troubled.

_____

_____

_____

_____

_____

_____

_____

_____

_____

# Day 3

# TOPIC: DO NOT BE AFRAID OF THE DARK

**Key Verse:** Psalm 139:12 "Indeed, the darkness shall not hide from You, but the night shines as the day; the darkness and the light are both alike to You."

During the writing of this devotional, I experienced a series of losses within my circle. Two of my uncles, one of my aunts, one cousin, and my best friend died over a short six-week period. There were moments when I was numb and other moments when my heart ached with pain. Even with my knowledge of the Cross and the promises of life after death, I cried and asked questions. How did God allow such painful events to occur so close together with little recovery time for our family? Doesn't God consider the timing of our trials? The world was crashing around my shoulders. I was in a dark place. Although God does not guarantee us a life free from pain, there are times when it is hard to accept the how, when, and why of life's events. The reality that my loved ones were no longer here and that we were unable to have a large funeral to celebrate their lives was at times unfathomable.

Occasionally, we all find ourselves in a dark place. When disappointment, grief, trouble, or health issues encircle our lives, we feel like we are in the dark. When we have lost our job, unable to pay the bills, bury our loved ones, get an unsettling diagnosis, or receive a phone call that makes our stomach drop, we feel like we are in the dark. Psalm 23 reminds us, *"when I walk through the valley of the shadow of death, I will fear no evil."* The shadow of death is probably a very dark place, but scripture reminds us that even when it seems dark to us, it is not dark to God. He sees everything and knows the path forward, even in the dark. Although my family and I experienced dark times, we comforted each other, held virtual memorials, and treasured every interaction we could have.

God's light empowers us to live a life of faith, even when things look dark. We must live life confidently, knowing the Light of God dwells in us and will sustain us even during difficult times. Researcher and renowned author Dr. Brené Brown writes, *"Only when we are brave enough to explore the darkness will we discover the infinite power of our light."* We know that our light comes from God within us. Declare the scripture, "The Lord is my Light and my salvation, whom shall I fear." (Psalm 27:1) We can enjoy this privilege and proclaim that we will no longer be afraid even when we face darkness.

**Prayer**: *Father, I will trust You even in situations that look dark. Heal my heart, mind and spirit from fear and make me confident and secure in You.*

## *fearLESS Thoughts*

Has God kept you through a dark period in your life? How can you use your past experiences to help you to deal with current fears?

_____

_____

_____

_____

_____

_____

_____

_____

_____

# Day 4

## TOPIC: THE PRIVILEGE TO PRAY

**Key Verse:** Philippians 4:6 "Do not be anxious about anything, but in every situation, by prayer and petition, with thanksgiving, present your requests to God."

Ms. Ruth was my Sunday School teacher as a teen. Anytime Ms. Ruth would pray, she would begin with, "Thank you God, for the privilege of prayer." She was intentional to thank God for the *privilege* to pray. That stuck with me! The definition of the word privilege is an exclusive right or advantage granted. In other words, a privilege is not something that you have to receive. Our perception of something impacts the way we approach it and the way we perceive prayer is important. Sometimes when our children fail to show appreciation for something that we do for them, we tell them, "This is a privilege, and we do not have to let you do this." I wonder if this is how God feels about our relationship to prayer. He has given us a vehicle where we can connect directly with Him. We do not need an appointment, and we can reach out to God at any time.

I guess all that we can do is pray. There is nothing left to do but pray. These phrases sound like a metaphorical "throwing in of the towel." How does God feel when we diminish him to a last resort? If we are in a position where all we can do is pray, we are in a good position, because prayer works. Let us stop minimizing this great gift that God has given to us. Prayer is a privilege. If we are dealing with fear and anxiety, we can communicate with God about it directly. Never feel that your problems are unimportant to God. He wants to hear from you and give you guidance for your life.

There are two ways to show someone that we appreciate a privilege they have granted us. First is to say, "Thank you," and the second is to use the privilege for its intended purpose. What a tremendous opportunity God has afforded us to be able to connect with Him in prayer. Commit today to use the privilege of prayer to ask God for wisdom in conquering your fears.

Place a chair in front of you before you pray today. Imagine that God is sitting in the chair listening to you. Let your prayer be a dialogue where you share with Him exactly what you are feeling and what causes you fear. Know that He is as close as the chair and that He hears you as you pray.

**Prayer:** *Lord, thank You that I can come to You in prayer about whatever concerns me. I commit to treasure the privilege to regularly connect with You.*

## *fearLESS Thoughts*

Is prayer sometimes taken for granted? How can you commit to making prayer more of a conversation and less of a monologue?

_____

_____

_____

_____

_____

_____

_____

_____

_____

# Day 5

## TOPIC: FEARS AS PAPER TIGERS

**Key Verse**: Isaiah 41:10 "Do not fear, for I am with you; do not be afraid, for I am your God. I will strengthen you; I will help you; I will uphold you with my victorious right hand."

Paper tiger is the literal English translation of the Chinese phrase *zhilaohu*. The term refers to something or someone that claims or appears to be powerful or threatening but is actually powerless. Many of us think that terrible things will happen if we face our fears. The truth is many of our fears are actually "paper tigers" and are nothing to fear. We give them power in our mind, but they have no real power. The more we focus on them, the more power they have. When we face our fears, we realize that many of them are only as dangerous and powerful as a paper tiger.

When I ventured into my educational consulting business, it took me over two years to quiet my fears. I was so terrified to fail that I was planning to fail. I told myself, "I am going to try this for a year, and then I will go back to a real job." I acted as if failure were a part of the plan so that when it happened, I would not be embarrassed or surprised. It did not matter that I had the support of my husband, encouragement from my friends and family, and a solid base of potential clients. I was still afraid. Throughout those two years, I made significant progress, yet my inner thoughts remained negative and fearful. Do I have what it takes to run my own business? Am I too young to serve as a consultant for large organizations and school districts? Should I wait until I earn a Ph.D.? Will I be able to generate enough income to plan for the future or will I compromise my family's lifestyle? My anxious thoughts and internal fears roared like a ferocious, undefeatable tiger.

Fear can rob us of our dreams and of the plans that God has for us. Sometimes this happens through an attack on our self-worth or our confidence. Through prayer, journaling, and a few weeks of counseling, I realized that my fears demonstrated a pessimistic view of myself and of God in me. God created me in His image, and therefore, as I was in doubt about myself, I was in doubt about the God in me. With God's blessings, constant prayer and hard work, my fears about my business have proven to be "paper tigers."  Is there a place in your life where the fear of what may happen has you paralyzed? Do not let paper tigers rob you of what God has for you. Step out in faith and live with the God-confidence that He has placed in you.

**Prayer**: *God, forgive me for doubting Your ability to work in and through me.  I commit to moving forward with the power, love, and sound mind that You have afforded me.*

## *fearLESS Thoughts*

Recall a time when you were afraid of something only to face it and realize that it was nothing to fear. How did you feel before and after the experience?

_____

_____

_____

_____

_____

_____

_____

_____

_____

# Day 6

## TOPIC: GIVE GOD YOUR FEARS

**Key Verse**: 1 Peter 5:7 "Cast all your anxiety on him because he cares for you."

The verb used in this verse, "to cast" or "Epirrhipto" in Greek, *means to throw upon or to fling something away from you.* Casting all our anxiety upon God includes our fears, worries, cares, and concerns.

We were not created to handle life on our own. God designed us to be dependent upon Him; so, we are to bring Him our concerns and allow Him to help with them. When we worry, our attention shifts from God and makes us blind to seeing His promises. Energy should be treated as a valuable commodity and more energy is spent when we worry than when we pray. Channel your energy in prayer today. We can pray about everything that concerns us. During His time on earth, Jesus prayed. He entrusted everything to God through prayer. We can do the same. God is all-caring, all-loving and his presence is ever-present. "He cares for you" is written in the present tense, meaning that, even right now, God cares for you. That is right; the almighty God cares for YOU!

My husband and I are great friends and I feel better when I tell him what's on my mind. We also have two adolescent children, who admit that they feel better when they talk about what is on their mind. After our conversations, nothing has changed, but we no longer feel we are carrying the burdens alone. We know that we are loved and that we are there for each other. We can have that same security by sharing our worries and fears with God. He will always be there for us.

Write items that are causing you concern or anxiety on a piece of paper. These may be current issues such as an upcoming job interview or a health concern. They could also be underlying concerns, such as not being good enough or wondering if you will find a spouse. Write them down and fold them into small squares. Place a basket or container a few feet in front of you and begin to fling each of them into the basket. (Do not use a trash can, for this may subconsciously send the message that your cares are unimportant. They are not.) You are merely casting your fears into the hands of a God who cares for you. Move through your day, knowing He cares about what concerns you.

**Prayer:** *Lord, I choose to cast my cares on You. I commit all my fears to You through prayer. I remember how much You care for me.*

## *fearLESS Thoughts*

Casting your anxiety on God means trusting Him to handle specific situations. In what specific situation do you have some anxiety?

_____

_____

_____

_____

_____

_____

_____

_____

_____

# Day 7

# TOPIC: EMBRACE THE UNKNOWN

**Key Verse**: 2 Corinthians 5:7 (NKJV) "For we walk by faith, not by sight."

Fear is usually associated with a level of uncertainty about something. We do not understand something, or we are not sure if it is going to turn out well. Not knowing something can be scary because we are most comfortable when we know (or think we know) exactly how things are going to turn out. Probably like you, I have had several seasons of uncertainty. These were also times of fear. I was uncertain that I would complete my degree since a class was not offered in my final semester. I was uncertain if I would find a wonderful man to marry and start a family. When my job ended, I was unsure if I could start my own business. I now realize that many of my greatest blessings have come following these seasons of uncertainty.

Sometimes we must be willing to embrace the unknown. We must be ready to move forward in life even though there may be some unanswered questions. The fact is, we are not able to handle knowing everything that will happen in our future. We might attempt to shift the events or make changes to our future. If I had known all the things that God had in store for my first 47 years of life, I would have run for the hills. I would have kindly informed God, "I'm not able to speak in front of large crowds. I am not qualified to serve in ministry. I am not going to be able to survive the loss of my dear friend. I do not like to write much, so the books you have planned for me to author are not going to happen." If I knew everything before they occurred, I would not have experienced an actual walk of faith. I would have sabotaged the blessings that God had for me.

We are living in uncertain times. No one knows exactly what the future will hold. Identify an area where you feel uncertain about how to move forward. Is there something that you have started, but fear has stalled your progress? Has paralysis developed out of the feeling of not knowing how things might turn out? Are you telling God all the reasons why something cannot happen? Realize that you will never achieve fearless living until you embrace the fact that you do not, will not, and do not need to know everything. We must be willing to walk by faith and not by sight. If we do only what we know how to do, we are not living fearlessly. We must be brave enough to admit when we do **not** know something. Then we will indeed be open to what God has in store and trust in His plan.

**Prayer:** *God, I am thankful that You know everything. I commit to walk in faith and watch as You make impossible things possible.*

## *fearLESS Thoughts*

When anxious about the future, I encourage you to declare something that you know for sure. For example, I know that God is still in control! I know that I can choose to be grateful. I know that God is always with me. What do you know for sure? Ask God to lead you and give you assurance.

_____

_____

_____

_____

_____

_____

_____

_____

_____

# Day 8

## TOPIC: EXCHANGE FEAR FOR TRUST

**Key Verse:** John 14:1 "Do not let your hearts be troubled. You believe in God; believe also in me."

Jesus' final words to His disciples at The Last Supper contains promises that are comforting. This scripture is often read at funerals and memorial services; however, this text is not only about life after death. It also has everything to do with our lives here and now. Jesus demonstrates His response to the disciples' fears with words of assurance. Jesus knew what was ahead, and He knew what was going on in the disciples' minds and hearts. They must have been disturbed, upset, and fearful. The ground must have been shifting beneath their feet. Jesus, their beloved teacher, was predicting His very own death and would be leaving them. In addition to announcing His departure to a place that they would not be able to follow, Jesus foretold His betrayal by Judas and imminent denial by Peter.

We often find that what is going on in the world will give us a reason to be disturbed. Things are uncertain, our routine has been compromised, and we are unable to see a path forward. This must be how the disciples felt when

Jesus was sharing the events that were to come. The One who they had been following was now preparing for His departure. Their world was about to be changed forever, yet in this troubling moment, He gives them this encouraging and affirming message. "Let not your heart be troubled. When they had to feel a level of uncertainty and fear about what was to come, we see Jesus comfort those closest to Him. These are the words of hope He gives to his disciples then and the same words that He is giving to us now. Despite everything that looks bad around them, Jesus promises them that His death will not be the end. When life has us feeling anxious or fearful about what is to come, hear Christ saying, "Let not your heart be troubled."

Trust in God. Trust is complete reliance on God. It is not just a feeling. It is when we put our actions, thoughts, emotions, hearts, and will in the direction that God would lead. God is the One for the troubled and fearful heart. He reminds us again and again that He is the One who will guide us through. Look at those places where you fear life is out of control, with your loved ones, with your job, or with your finances. Choose to exchange your fearful and troubled heart for active reliance on God. Choose with each moment not to have a troubled heart. Each day remember the promises of Christ and do not let your heart be troubled.

**Prayer**: *Lord, we thank you for your words of assurance that remind us that you have already overcome the world. Give us the peace that we need to trust You, even when times are difficult.*

## *fearLESS Thoughts*

Meditation, deep breathing, prayer, mindfulness practices help to focus our thoughts and feelings. On this journey to #fearLESS living, what do you do to help control your emotions?

_____

_____

_____

_____

_____

_____

_____

_____

_____

# Day 9

## TOPIC: FEED YOUR FAITH

**Key Verse**: Philippians 4: 8 "Finally, brethren, whatever things are true, whatever things are noble, whatever things are just, whatever things are pure, whatever things are lovely, whatever things are of good report, if there is any virtue and if there is anything praiseworthy—meditate on these things."

There is a story of a man who had two dogs. He would race these dogs each week, and people in the town would come to watch and bet on which dog would win the race. Each week, a different dog would win. There seemed to be no consistency in which dog would win the race from week to week. The owner would also place his bet and was always able to predict which dog would win. He was the only one who could correctly guess the winner of the race. After weeks of losing money, the townspeople asked the owner, How do you always know which dog will win the race? His response, It is really pretty easy. The week before the race, I feed one dog and starve the other. The dog I feed will win. I know that when you feed something, it gets stronger, and when you starve something, it loses strength.

If we want to minimize the impact of fear in our lives, we must be intentional about feeding our faith. In the days surrounding the September 11th terrorist attacks and the COVID-19 pandemic, the news feed was flooded with replays and reports of disturbing information. Continuing to watch these news broadcasts got to the point where I was feeding my fears. Visuals and projections of death and future attacks caused a level of anxiety that bordered traumatic. I had to limit the intake of fearful information and spend more time with God. If we want to have peace, we must feed our faith more than our fears. We feed our fears when we focus on our problems or the problems of the world. We feed our faith when we focus on what God has promised us in His Word.

Feed your faith by reading the Word of God. Philippians 4:8 reminds us each day that we are to think about whatever is true, whatever is noble, whatever is right, whatever is pure, whatever is lovely, whatever is admirable, and anything excellent or praiseworthy. Whatever is causing us to be afraid probably will not make the cut. Be intentional today and focus on positive things. Confess positively and live positively. Connect with people who can help you as you courageously starve your fears. How else will you starve your fears and feed your faith in the days ahead? Create a plan for how you will minimize focusing on what leads to anxious thoughts and maximize opportunities to encourage your faith.

**Prayer:** *Father, help me to feed my faith over my fears. Let Your Word guide me and help me to surround myself with positive people.*

## *fearLESS Thoughts*

We must fill our circle with those who can help us to feed our faith. Write down the names of people that you can call on that fit this description. Your list might include your pastor, family member, friend, or even a spiritual or motivational leader.

_____

_____

_____

_____

_____

_____

_____

_____

_____

# Day 10

## TOPIC: GOD IS...

**Key Verse**: Psalm 46:1 "God is our refuge and strength, an ever-present help in trouble."

A refuge is a place to hide and a place of safety when things around us get tough. It is where we go when we need to be covered. Just like an umbrella in the rain, God shields and protects us. Psalm 46:1 does not say that He *provides us* with a refuge and a source of strength. It says that He *is* our refuge and our strength.

We cannot be ignorant of the dangers that exist in this world. Violence, racial tension, wars, and disease are all around. However, there is only one place believers can find *real* security and protection. We have hope as God as our refuge, a place we can run to for protection from life's unexpected and scary moments. When life has us feeling fearful, God is a constant place of refuge. He is our safe place. God never said that our lives would be without trouble. John 16:33 says quite the opposite; "In this world, you will have trouble." We will experience disappointments, losses, illness, and struggle with relationships. Yet through these challenging times, we must hold to the second half of this scripture, "But take heart! I have overcome the world."

Make Psalm 46:1 a personal proclamation. God is <u>my</u> refuge and strength; an ever-present help when I am in trouble. Notice if your mood shifts as you boldly proclaim this truth. Repeat this scripture to provide yourself with confidence and strength. With everything that is going on in the world and with all the unknowns on the agenda for the years to come, we should repeatedly state and embrace God's promises. God will guard us against dangers seen and unseen. Psalm 46 ends with a command to "be still and know that I am God." What comfort! Taking refuge in God, be still, and know that He is God. He is our protector, and although there will be storms, God promises to keep us under His covering. Rest in God and allow Him to show Himself strong. Trouble can happen at any time, but with God as our refuge, the chaos around us will not override the calm within us.

**Prayer:** *God, I am thankful that You are ever-present. Remind me today to be still and to know that You are my safe place.*

## *fearLESS Thoughts*

Where are some places you typically run for refuge when you are feeling anxious? Your phone? A friend? Burying yourself in work? How is God a far more secure shelter than the other places we look for refuge?

_____

_____

_____

_____

_____

_____

_____

_____

# Day 11

## TOPIC: FEAR WILL NOT WIN

**Key Verse**: 1 John 4:4 "You, dear children, are from God and have overcome them because the One who is in you is greater than the one who is in the world."

Think of the things that cause you to fear. Do you believe they frighten God? Imagine God saying to Moses, "I do not know if we can outrun Pharaoh. He and his army are pretty fast" or to David, "I am going to be with you, but Goliath is pretty big, so I'm not sure my power is enough." Was God intimidated by these powerful figures? Can you imagine God cowering in fear against your enemy or your situation? If the answer is "no," then you have no reason to fear.

God did not intend for us to run from our fears. His plan was and still is for us to confront any issue in our lives with confidence. God is on our side, and therefore, our confidence is in Him. With God's abiding presence, we can move on despite our fears. There might be battles to fight, mountains to conquer, or obstacles to overcome; but God has promised to always be with us. We are not to fear; neither should we be intimidated by any challenge. We are to face them head-on because the greater One is with us.

Fear is not from God, and it is not more powerful than God. God knew that fear would come and attempt to rob us of our peace. Fear makes us feel that we are far away from God. It tells us that we are on our own, and there is no one to help. Fear whispers in our ears that God is not concerned about us, and it makes our "giants" appear undefeatable. The truth is, God is all-mighty and powerful. He is omniscient, omnipresent, and omnipotent. There is nothing that He cannot do because all power belongs to Him. He does not get tired or need to take a day off. He is always present, able to deliver, and available to answer His children when we call. Today, walk with God-confidence; because "greater is He that is within you than he that in the world." God has equipped you to defeat fear and to walk in faith. Declare today that fear will not win!

**Prayer:** *God, I believe that You are greater than all my problems. I am assured today that You are always with me. Because of that, I will not be afraid.*

# *fearLESS Thoughts*

*We are at the halfway point in this devotional. It is important to review your progress and plan for the future. What have you done recently, or will you do in the upcoming days to demonstrate that you are fearLESS?*

_____

_____

_____

_____

_____

_____

_____

_____

_____

# Day 12

# TOPIC: DEVELOP A HUMBLE HEART

*Key Verse: 1 Peter 5:6* "Humble yourselves, therefore, under God's mighty hand, that He may lift you up in due time."

A pilot, a child, a politician, and a minister were on an airplane. The plane began to experience trouble, and it started to dive. With only three parachutes and not much time to spare, a decision had to be made about who would use the parachutes. The pilot said, "I have a wife and four children and can't leave them alone, so I deserve a parachute." The pilot quickly took a parachute and jumped out of the plane. The politician quickly spoke up, "I am important and do good work for many people, so I deserve to live." He assertively grabbed a parachute and jumped out of the plane. The minister looked at the child and graciously said, "You have your whole life to live, so you should take the last parachute." The child, looking back at the minister who just made a humble offering, replied, "Thank you, sir, but the politician just grabbed my backpack. Both of us can have a parachute."

I used to think that humility was thinking less of yourself. It does not nor does it mean that you are unimportant. It means that you realize the world does not revolve around you. If you are humble, you are comfortable with your place in the world. A humble person accepts their position as a part of a larger plan. Humility is a crucial ingredient in sincere prayer. A humble heart is concerned about God's desires for our lives and the lives of others. When our prayers are only for our needs, we are not showing humility. Humble prayers are not just "bless me and meet my needs" but include "bless others and meet their needs." True humility before God yields our desires to His.

If we could overcome fear and solve our problems on our own, why would we need God? Before we can experience God's intervention, we must demonstrate a genuine level of humility. We must invite him into our lives. If we are to overcome fear, we must acknowledge that we need God's help. God derives pleasure in helping and caring for humble people yet frowns and rejects those who are full of pride and arrogance. When we humble ourselves before God, we make room for God to move; we accept that He is greater and sovereign over everything. Humble yourself before God, allow Him to help you overcome your fears, and ask Him to help you see yourself as part of His great plan.

Today, position yourself in prayer and model humility. Pray on your knees. Bow your head with your palms open or lie face down. Demonstrate your complete surrender and humble submission before God. Take time to be quiet before Him. Ask Him to speak to you.

**Prayer**: *God, I acknowledge that I can do nothing without you. I humble myself before You. Thank You for using me as a part of Your greater plan.*

## *fearLESS Thoughts*

A humble heart is concerned for others. For whom are you praying for today? Write their name or their role in your life. (my neighbor, my mother, my boss, the President, etc.)

_____

_____

_____

_____

_____

_____

_____

_____

_____

# Day 13

# TOPIC: CALL 9-1-1

**Key Verse:** Psalm 91:1(NKJV) "He who dwells in the secret place of the Most High, shall abide under the shadow of the Almighty."

When you think of 911, you probably think of the emergency number or a call for urgent help. It is what we call upon when we are in need or need help. When we dial 911, we want someone to answer. It would not make sense for emergency services to have regular business hours or only be available Monday thru Friday. Emergencies can and will happen at any time, and we want to know that help is always available. Just like emergency services, God does not have office hours. He is available mornings, afternoons, evenings, and weekends and does not get overwhelmed with a surge of calls. He can answer everyone's call simultaneously. He is ever-present!

It is clear why Psalm 91:1 is often referred to as the 9-1-1 verse. It provides immediate comfort to life's fears. God has provided us a secret place that is free of stress, fear and worry. Here is where He has promised to give us protection, comfort, love, and arms to shield us. The entire 91st Psalm is filled with declarations of the goodness and power of God. Psalm 91:1 was my grandmother's favorite scripture. She memorized it, quoted it regularly, and lived a life knowing that God was her place of shelter.

Do you have a place where you go to have a special connection with God? It may be a special chair in your home, a park in your neighborhood, or even in the shower. Go to your secret place and read the entire 91st Psalm. Focus on the last two verses that reveal to us why we do not have to fear. If we abide in the secret place of prayer, God will keep us covered. When we feel there is a 911 situation in life and we need to make an urgent call for help, remember Psalm **91:1**. Allow God to provide you the help, the protection, and assurance only found in His secret place.

**Prayer:**  *Heavenly Father, I come to You today and hide in your secret place. Be my shield and my security. I thank You because I call upon your Word in Psalm 91:1 and know that You have me covered.*

# *fearLESS Thoughts*

Where is your secret place?  Identify a location and create a schedule for when you will connect with God.

_____

_____

_____

_____

_____

_____

_____

_____

_____

# Day 14

## TOPIC: GOD CAN HANDLE IT

**Key Verse**: Matthew 28:5-6 "The angel said to the women, 'Do not be afraid, for I know that you are looking for Jesus, who was crucified. He is not here; He has risen, just as He said'."

A cemetery at the break of day would qualify as a place where I might be a little frightened. Following the crucifixion of Jesus, this is precisely where we find several women who have traveled to His tomb. The women faced darkness, armed guards and a large boulder designed to block the place where Jesus' body laid. Yet, they ventured to the gravesite despite what scary things might be ahead. When I imagine this scene, I wonder if I would have made it. It reads like an episode of Fear Factor. I may have chosen to wait for CNN, FOX News, a Tweet, a Snap, a Facebook post, or the latest edition of the Gethsemane Gazette to learn of Jesus' whereabouts. When they arrived at the empty tomb, the guards were immobilized, the stone was rolled away, and an angel told them, "Do not be afraid." The women at the tomb were also afraid because this was all new to them. They had seen God's power before but never like this. Then after seeing the resurrected Jesus, the women leave the tomb "with fear and great joy."

The moment the women would be most afraid is when God steps in. He sends His angel, provides comfort, and handles everything. He handled the guards, and He handled the stone that blocked the tomb. God handled it all and Jesus rose from the dead.   God can also handle whatever situation is keeping us up at night, increasing our blood pressure, or making our stomach uneasy. God can handle whatever is causing us fear. If our situation needs to be changed, God can handle it. If a pandemic is spreading, God can handle it. If surgeons need to be used, God can handle it. If chemotherapy is in the plan, God can handle it. It is not God's desire for us to be afraid of every piece of bad news, every diagnosis, or every enemy. He wants us to know that He can handle everything.   No matter what has you afraid, worried, or upset, trust that God can handle it. Because if God has conquered death, everything else on your list is easy.

**Prayer:** *Father, I thank you for the reminder that I do not need to be afraid.   I trust that you can handle whatever situation is causing me fear.*

## *fearLESS Thoughts*

We do not usually hear about people being afraid and joyful at the same time. It is always one or the other. However, many of life's moments can contain both fear and great joy.  New job, new baby, new opportunity...Fear and great joy.  What personal experiences would you describe as containing fear and great joy?

_____

_____

_____

_____

_____

_____

_____

_____

_____

# Day 15

# TOPIC: TREASURE GOD'S PRESENCE

**Key Verse***:* Deuteronomy 31:8 "The Lord Himself goes before you and will be with you; he will never leave you nor forsake you. Do not be afraid; do not be discouraged."

My Aunt Kathy recently celebrated a milestone birthday. She invited many of her family and friends over for a house party to celebrate her special day. We asked her for gift ideas to share with those who were attending the special event. Her response was for us not to buy her anything and simply know that our *presence* would be the best *presen*t she could receive. She did not desire material gifts because, as most of us will eventually realize, having someone spend time with you is truly an invaluable gift.

The same is true in our daily walk as we conquer our fears. God's presence is the best present we have. In Exodus 33, Moses says to God, "If Your presence does not go with us, do not send us up from here." He understood the blessing of God's presence, and he craved it. Moses had earlier proclaimed Joshua to be his successor. He knew that Joshua would face many challenges on the way, so he encouraged Joshua by telling him that the Lord would be with him. Based on this promise of God's presence, Joshua could cross Jordan, overcome Jericho, and conquer Canaan's land. (Joshua 2) In the New Testament, Jesus reiterated, "Lo, I am with you, always, even unto the end of the world." (Matthew 28:20) Accepting God's promise of divine presence will help us not to live a life of fear. God knows that all our days will not be smooth and trouble-free, so He promised to always be with us. Therefore, we must believe this great promise, pray with this promise, and live in the reality of this promise.

How would you feel if every time you spoke to a friend or loved one, they always wanted something from you? I know I would not be excited to hear from them, and I might neglect to answer their call or respond to their text. Think about your most recent prayers. Do they mainly consist of requests for blessings and "gifts" from God? Are they primarily focused on you and your desires? Today, be intentional to spend a significant amount of time thanking the Lord for His presence in your life and the lives of your loved ones. Demonstrate that you are profoundly grateful for God's promise to always be with you. Commit to asking God for nothing. Let your prayer time solely include prayers of thanksgiving. Take notice if this feels vastly different from your regular prayers. If it does, thank Him that even when we selfishly only ask for blessings or only pray for ourselves, He never neglects our call.

**Prayer:** *Father, I believe, and thank You for the promise of Your Divine presence. I commit to valuing You and Your presence over any present that You could give me.*

## *fearLESS Thoughts*

God enjoys hearing our thanksgiving and our gratitude. What are you grateful for today? Take a full 5 minutes and make a list of all that you are grateful for today.

_____

_____

_____

_____

_____

_____

_____

_____

_____

# Day 16

## TOPIC: TRUST IN GOD

**Key Verse**: Psalm 56:3 "When I am afraid, I put my trust in you."

My family has a favorite auto mechanic. When our cars have issues, he is the first person we call because we trust his skill and knowledge. We have confidence that he has the expertise to repair all sorts of mechanical problems. As we drive about, if we have any trouble with our vehicles, we have someone we can rely on. We would not go to someone without the skill or ability to help in our time of need. When we are afraid, on some level, our mind doubts God. More specifically, we doubt His ability to handle whatever is triggering our fear. Imagine how free we would feel if we learned to genuinely believe that all we needed to do was to trust in God.

I used to think that trust was just saying, "Oh, I guess it will come out all right." Trust does not mean closing our eyes to the world and the dangers and hardships we face. It is not about having "blind faith," but knowing who has the answers. Trust looks at things as they are and looks at God as He is. When we trust in God, it causes our moments of anxiety and fear to be short-lived. The Bible illustrates time and again that God has the skill, knowledge, and experience to handle whatever we fear. God has a Ph.D. in everything! Nothing we can bring to Him is beyond His knowledge and understanding.

Who is God? Have you ever really thought about it? My Pastor, Rev. Howard K. Hammond, shares a simple yet powerful definition of God. God is the Creator and Sustainer of the Universe. We get to trust in God who is the One that causes the days and nights to exist, the One who places the sun and moon in the sky, the One who gives us air to breathe, and a heart that beats. Yes, this God is more than able to handle any problem, concern, or fear. Trust me; if we compare our fears to God's power, they will not be able to match up. Rest in the arms of the God who is the Creator and Sustainer of the Universe. He has given us divine assurance of His presence and constant help. Trust in God. It is the safest thing that you can ever do.

**Prayer:** *Father, forgive me for underestimating and doubting Your power; I trust You and know that You can handle everything I bring before You.*

# *fearLESS Thoughts*

In what areas of your life have you demonstrated that you trust God?  In what areas can you trust God more?

_____

_____

_____

_____

_____

_____

_____

_____

_____

# Day 17

# TOPIC: RENAME AND REFRAME

**Key Verse**: Isaiah 62:2 "You will be called by a new name that the mouth of the LORD will bestow."

Ten years after the September 11th terrorists attack, NY Mayor Michael Bloomberg stood at the place known as Ground Zero. He said, "We will never forget the devastation to the area that came to be known as Ground Zero. Never. But the time has come to call those 16 acres what they are: The World Trade Centre and the National September 11th Memorial and Museum." He recognized the importance of renaming and reframing places and events that have caused us fear and heartache. With the motivation to rebuild, Mr. Bloomberg wanted to shift our attention from the devastation that occurred.

The words we use to describe our times of hurt, loss, or fear matter. Instead of referring to the lost job, can it be the job that taught you new skills? Instead of the relationship that ended painfully, is it the period when you learned something about yourself? Words matter and intentional reframing can be a powerful tool in developing resilience in the face of our fears. Have you ever considered that God can give you a new perspective of it if you revisit your disappointment? Your past can become a testimony to help others. Reframing can also lead to redefining. When we define something as one thing, it no longer defines it as something else. If I am a survivor, then I am no longer a victim. If I am a success, then I am not a failure. We must not only identify who we are when we choose to live fearlessly, but we must also decide who we are not.

Our past may contain our own ground zeros. Our ground zeros are places where we feel defeated, where hurt has occurred, or where there are memories of what was that is now lost. Today, I encourage you to rename some places and events that tell you not what you have lost but what you have gained. Have you gained the strength to move on? Are you better, more loving, more resilient, and more purposeful? Do you have a new appreciation for the people and things in your life? If not, pray that God will help you realize all that you have gained. Rename your ground zeros so that you will never again allow that place or space to bring you to a place of fear and defeat.

Identify what could be a ground zero in your life. It may be a date on the calendar, a previous relationship, an unfinished project, or a former job. Remember not to be afraid of memories or thoughts; they are part of what you bring to your future. Ask for God's guidance in renaming this time or place and helping you move forward in all that He has for you.

**Prayer**: *Heavenly Father, help me to reframe and move past my places of fear or hurt so that I may better serve you.*

## *fearLESS Thoughts*

Fear keeps us looking back and often keeps us from moving forward. Have memories of past experiences ever kept you from moving forward? How can you rename and reframe the experience?

_____

_____

_____

_____

_____

_____

_____

_____

_____

# Day 18

# TOPIC: FROM FEAR TO GREAT BLESSINGS

**Key Verse:** Jeremiah 29:11 *"For I know the plans I have for you' declares the Lord plans to prosper you and not to harm you, plans to give you hope and a future."*

For several years, I served on the Board of Directors for a private Christian school. In 2010, our principal accepted another position, and the school was without a leader. After an invitation and much prayer, I stepped away from my public-school job to serve as the school principal. Excited, yet fearful, about the work ahead, I moved forward as the school's leader. The school was wonderful and full of committed educators who loved and prayed for our students. At the end of our 19th year, we were making plans for our 20th school year in a big way: new technology, new staff, and a new curriculum. Unfortunately, there was a significant shift in the economy. Families were losing their jobs and having to make tough decisions about which priorities to maintain. For many, private school was a luxury, they could no longer afford. Within a few months, it was clear that many of our students would not be returning in the fall, and our enrollment plummeted. We had no choice but to notify parents, children, and staff that our school would be closing.

The pain I felt was enormous. I wondered what I had done wrong. The school was doing well, but it closed while under my leadership. As I watched our teachers pack up their things and I emptied my office, I felt a level of guilt and failure that is difficult to describe. The school became *my* ground zero. I did not want to see it. It hurt too much to remember the faces of those who were once excited to walk through the doors and were now having to find a new school or place to work. A leap of faith that was now appearing as a significant failure.

Sometimes we look at challenging times in our lives and think that God has abandoned us. Little do we know that God has set us up for a major blessing. Although Renaissance Christian Academy reminded me of disappointment and loss, God has since led me on an amazing new path. He has allowed me to serve educators nationally and internationally, to teach and preach His Word, and my former school continues as a place of ministry.

The term "ground zero" did not originate from the September 11th attacks. It was a term used to refer to any point of a dramatic event. We do not have to forget what happened at our personal ground zeros, but we should see more than hurt or loss. Your past does not have to be the same as your future. Encourage yourself to see beyond your ground zeros so that you may move forward with God's plan for your future. Do not look at where you are or where you have been; look at where you are headed. God will give you a hope and a future.

**Prayer:** *Lord, help me realize that sometimes the places where we experienced great fear or hurt may also be the places of our greatest blessings.*

## *fearLESS Thoughts*

Where do you hope to be standing in the next five years? How can lessons learned in the past help you to move forward?

_____

_____

_____

_____

_____

_____

_____

_____

_____

# Day 19

# TOPIC: ASK FOR GOD'S GUIDANCE

**Key Verse:** Proverbs 3:5-6 (NJKV) "Trust in the Lord with all your heart and lean not on your own understanding; in all your ways acknowledge Him, and He shall direct your paths."

In my line of work, I make several road trips. When I travel to an unknown destination for the first time, I make sure that I am prepared. I put the address into my navigation system. I find a major chain hotel in the area. I also research the local news in that city. This helps ensure I avoid hazardous driving conditions and enjoy my stay. Mostly, it prevents me from getting lost.

Although I do my best to create a safety plan as I travel, my greatest trust is in God. He has the ultimate safety plan for the whole universe in His hands. He knows the beginning from the end and how all events will transpire. God knows what is best for me and I trust Him to keep me safe. There have been times when the Holy Spirit has nudged me to leave a town following a presentation or to stay and enjoy a dinner invitation with my host. God is always there to guide me. The more I connect with Him, the clearer I hear His words of guidance for my life.

When the Amalekites invaded Ziklag and took all that David had, David consulted the LORD before fighting them. (1 Samuel 29) It was after God gave him the go-ahead order that he conquered and recovered everything he lost. Each morning, before we do anything, we should acknowledge and invite God to guide our footsteps. Do not isolate God from your decisions, the small ones or the big ones. There is nothing unimportant to God, and He can help guide us in all our ways. Imagine what a day would be like when you asked God to guide each of your steps. Not just a general prayer for guidance, but specific directions for all that you do. Today, take a couple of minutes before you pray and write down all the decisions that you may have to make. Direction is essential, for without it, we get lost. Pray over your list and ask God to direct your path.

**Prayer:** *Father, I acknowledge you in every area of my life today, be the decision-maker in all that I venture to do.*

## *fearLESS Thoughts*

In what areas of your life have you followed God's guidance? In what areas do you need more guidance? What do you sense God leading you to do at this point in your life?

_____

_____

_____

_____

_____

_____

_____

_____

_____

# Day 20

## TOPIC: LISTEN TO GOD'S DIRECTIONS

**Key Verse:** Psalm 32:8 "I will instruct you and teach you in the way you should go; I will counsel you with my eye upon you."

Pay attention, listen carefully, wash your hands, and say thank you. There are reminders that I give my children regularly. Although they have heard me tell them quite a bit, they occasionally forget. As they mature and grow, I hope that they need fewer reminders and can hear my words in their heads. I wonder if this is how God feels about us, as we are called to "hide His Word in our hearts." (Psalm 119:11)

In surveying the Bible, we see God giving the same reminders repeatedly. He issues the command, "Do not be afraid," over 200 times! When Abram left his father's house, God says, "Do not be afraid." (Gen 12) When God prepares to send Moses to Pharaoh, he tells him, "Do not be afraid." (Exodus 3) When the children of Israel prepare to go to the Promised Land, God gives the commandment through Moses, "Do not be afraid." (Deuteronomy 1) When Joshua steps up to leadership after Moses, God repeatedly tells him, "Do not be afraid." (Joshua 1:9)

When the angel comes down to Bethlehem to tell Mary about Jesus, he says, "Do not be afraid." (Luke 1:30) When Jesus walks to the disciples in the middle of the water during the storm, He says, "Do not be afraid." (John 6:20) The repeating of this directive by God definitively tells us two things. First, God does not want us to be afraid, and second, we need regular reminders NOT to do so.

God desires to bring us closer to Him. A place where we hear His voice saying, "this is the way, walk in it." By listening to God's voice through His Word, we extend our understanding and deepen our intimacy with Him. There are so many heartaches, difficulties, and troubles that can be avoided in our lives when we listen to God. He knows what is best for our lives. Today, meditate on God's words of direction. Picture Him holding you in His arms, whispering, "Do not be afraid."

**Prayer:** *God, I hear you telling me not to be afraid. Help me move forward with what You have called me to do, and I thank you that Your eye will be upon me.*

## *fearLESS Thoughts*

Fear keeps up from attempting and accomplishing many things in life. What would you do if you were not afraid?

_____

_____

_____

_____

_____

_____

_____

_____

_____

# Day 21

## TOPIC: FEARLESS-THE COMMAND

**Key Verse**: Joshua 1:9 "Have I not commanded you? Be strong and courageous. Do not be afraid; do not be discouraged; for the LORD, your God will be with you wherever you go."

I used to think that I had to wait until I was entirely without doubt, anxiety, or fear before moving forward with what God had for me. If we expect never to be afraid of anything, we will probably not accomplish very much. Have you ever said, "I will wait until I feel more confident before I do that?" God has empowered each of us for fearless living today.

Pastor Tony Evans says that faith is living as if God was telling you the truth. We see Joshua live in this way. God approaches Joshua, Moses' successor, and assures him that He has a plan for his future. God commanded Joshua to be fearless and courageous. Courage is only needed when fear is present. God knew that Joshua might experience fear and told him to be courageous despite his fear. God, too, has a plan for your future. Have faith and live as if God is telling you the truth. Fear is a complicated emotion. It can motivate us, or it can paralyze us. We must choose how we respond to it. When you find yourself in situations that expose your fears, remember the promises of God and be courageous despite your fear. Do it afraid! Do it scared! Just do it!

Reread today's key verse. Hear God repeating these same words to you today. Imagine His earlier whisper is now in the firmer tone of a parent helping you to escape from the window of a burning home. "Do not be afraid. Trust Me. I would never let you fall. Just jump into my arms. I've got you." It is a loving voice, yet it is also critical that you heed His command. God wants us to trust Him, knowing that He has us covered. Move fearlessly into His purpose for your life by using the three offensive weapons Paul speaks of in 2 Timothy 1:7. I can confidently say that this scripture no longer challenges my faith but equips me to move forward. When we are attacked by fear, 2 Timothy 1:7 tells us that we have been more than equipped to overcome its effect by using the power, love, and sound mind that God has graciously given us.

**Prayer**: *God, please continue to give me the power to live a fearless life. I will no longer focus on what causes me fear, but rather focus on the power of God, who gives me the strength to face my fear. I believe that I am empowered for fearless living. I declare that I will walk in your love and trust you with my life from this day forward. I do not have to live with fear.* I will remember your promises and depend on your presence as I walk fearlessly into my future. Amen.

# fearLESS Thoughts

Review and reflect on all that you have read and learned. Take the time to revel in the ways you have encountered God in the past 21 days.

_____

_____

_____

_____

_____

_____

_____

_____

_____

# About The Author

Shauna F. King is an educator, author, and speaker. She serves as an Associate Minister at Springdale Community Church in Springdale, MD. She is also the Executive Director of King Professional Development Services, which provides keynotes and workshops for schools and child-serving organizations. She and her husband, Mark, have two school age children and reside in Maryland. She is also the author of School Smart: It's More Than Just Reading and Writing.

Follow her on Twitter at @shaunafking or email her at shaunafking@gmail.com.

Made in the USA
Monee, IL
09 February 2021

60070899R10049